By Hand or by Heart

S Lynn G

Preface

Jealousy… Envy…Greed…Selfishness. They all lead to the root of bitterness, then on to murder. Yes, dear friend, I said, "MURDER!" Murder has become a common way of life in today's society. You say, "No, it hasn't. I haven't committed murder; in fact, I do not even know a murderer." Well, yes, it has become a way of life for a lot of people. We hear about it on the radio and television. We read about in the newspapers every single day, and some have even seen it in their own neighborhoods. Chances are you have committed murder too but refuse to recognize it–perhaps not with your hands, but in your heart. Jealousy is so damaging, and affects so many people in so many ways.

Because there is nothing new under the sun we can read in the Bible and see the devastation jealousy has left in its wake–all the way back to the very beginning of time. The only difference between then and now is, that was then, involving those people, and this is now, involving us. It doesn't make a bit of difference that thousands of years have passed or that the folks back then didn't have all the modern conveniences we have today. The fact is, people are people, and we are sinners. Throughout the Bible we see jealousy and its destruction; it is so exceedingly harmful to anyone whose life it touches.

Dedication

To my wonderful husband for always encouraging me no matter how I am attempting to serve our Lord.

To my loving sisters who allowed me to expose our dysfunctional family in a public way.

To the fabulous Christian woman who edited this book for me. I will be eternally grateful to her for taking the time out of her very busy schedule and for her incredible expertise.

To my remarkable additional family and friends who stuck by me as I struggled through writing this book.

I thank God for all of you; may He bless each one of you in a very special way.

Contents

Chapter 1

SIN

Webster's Elementary Dictionary for Boys and Girls definition
of *sin*, a verb; "to break the law of God."

I was talking with one of my sisters, and I was curious to
know why she had been jealous as a child. I asked her, and
without airing all of our family's dirty laundry for the rest of
the world to see, I will put it like she did–we were a dysfunctional family. In her opinion we were disconnected.

I am not fond of the word *dysfunctional*; it just sounds
so "yikesie," but according to the definition, I have to agree
with her because it means "the inability to relate emotionally with each other." The news is out: we were nothing like
the families of Ozzie and Harriet Nelson or Ward and June
Cleaver. Dysfunctional families have been around since the
beginning of time, and they can be found at 123 Main Street,
Anywhere, U.S.A. If the truth be known, they can be found
at 456 Central Avenue, Anywhere, The World. As a matter of
fact, the first dysfunctional family took place just outside the
Garden of Eden. It really doesn't matter where the dysfunctional family lives because it is not where, but how they live
that is the real problem.

We could all be living in Paradise right this very moment if Adam and Eve would have followed God's command. And they did for the most part, but God is not looking for just **part** of what He tells us to be taken seriously. He is looking for **every word** He tells us to be taken seriously. God had told Adam to dress and keep the Garden. God also told Adam he could freely eat from every tree, except from the tree of knowledge of good and evil, which grew in the midst of the Garden. God made it very plain what would happen if he did, that being he would surely die.

Adam and Eve must have lived a life of ease in the Garden, though not a drop of rain had fallen as of yet. The greenhouse effect kept the Garden perfectly moisturized. The weeds had not been introduced, so there was none of that back-breaking work to do. There might have been some pruning, but for the most part the Garden was for their food, a place to call home, and where they communed with God in the cool of the day.

Then in *Genesis chapter 3* it happened: Eve disobeyed God. Who knows just exactly how the conversation between Eve and the serpent got started, but we all know how it ended. Eve listened to the deceptive words of the serpent, and then she actually ate of the fruit from the tree from which God had forbidden them to eat. Not only did she go against what God had commanded, but she involved her husband. She gave to Adam, and he did eat also. They both had committed the very first sin against God. Can you imagine what they must have been thinking when they noticed they were naked? It couldn't have been all that fabulous because they were ashamed and did not want God to see them that way, so they got busy trying to cover up the obvious.

When Adam and Eve heard the voice of the LORD God walking in the Garden in the cool of the day, they tried to hide from Him. Of course, the flimsy aprons they had made out of fig leaves were useless, so they tried hiding themselves amongst the trees, but that didn't work either because it is impossible to hide from God.

When Adam heard God calling his name, he was probably thinking the same thing we would be thinking, OH NO, I'M IN TROUBLE NOW! Honestly, for the most part, we know when we have sinned and when we are in trouble with God. God knew they were hiding from Him, but He asked Adam anyway. "Adam, where art thou?" God always gives us an opportunity to confess our sins in order to make things right. Notice, God came asking, not accusing.

Adam was truthful when he confessed he was hiding because he was naked and ashamed. But when God asked Adam who had told him he was naked and asked if he had eaten from the tree of knowledge of good and evil, Adam stopped short of accountability. The answer to that question should have been, "Yes, I did eat from that tree." Instead, neither Adam nor Eve confessed their sin, and they made matters worse when Adam blamed God and Eve blamed the serpent. The same thing is still happening today. Nobody wants to be held accountable for his sin, and of course it is always someone else's fault.

Wow, does that mean God lied? Adam and Eve didn't die when they ate of the fruit like He said they would. No, God did not lie then, nor will He ever. God is and will always be pure, sinless, and perfect in every way. Adam and Eve did not die physically but spiritually the moment they ate of the fruit. Because of their sin against God, there were immediate consequences that followed their actions. God cursed the serpent above every beast of the field. *Genesis 3:14b says, "...upon thy belly shalt thou go, and dust shalt thou eat all the days of thy life."* God also said this to the serpent, in *Genesis 3:15, "And I will put enmity between thee and the woman, and between thy seed and her seed; it shall bruise thy head, and thou shalt bruise his heel." Enmity* means "hostility, hatred, intense aggression or anger, and strong opposition."

There was a curse put upon Adam and Eve too. The woman's curse was not just to Eve, but to all women. *Genesis 3:16* says, *"Unto the woman he said, I will greatly multiply thy sorrow and thy conception; in sorrow thou shalt bring forth children; and thy desire shall be to thy husband, and he shall rule over thee."* So now we know why there is so much pain involved in child birth. We can thank Eve for it all, not only for the pain and sorrow, but for God's placing our husband as the head of the household. God set the guidelines for the running of the perfect home right here in Genesis all because Eve was weak; she listened to the deceptive words of Satan as he appealed to her vanity, and she fulfilled the desire of her heart instead of following every word of God's command.

Likewise, the man's curse was not just to Adam; it was for all men. *Genesis 3:17, 18* says, *"And unto Adam he said, Because thou hast hearkened unto the voice of thy wife, and hast eaten of the tree, of which I commanded thee, saying, Thou shalt not eat of it: cursed is the ground for thy sake; in sorrow shalt thou eat of it all the days of thy life; Thorns also and thistles shall it bring forth to thee; and thou shalt eat the herb of the field."* Not only was Adam cursed, but the ground was also, which stands to reason because God formed Adam from the dust of the ground, and when He breathed the breath of life into Adam, Adam became a living soul.

From that point on, Adam was going to have to work by the sweat of his brow. Can you believe it? With just one taste of the forbidden fruit, Adam went from a groundskeeper, to a full-fledged farmer. He would now have to till the ground in order to plant the seeds. He would have to wait months for his crops to come in. There would be a time of harvest and preparation for his food from a ground cursed with thorns and thistles, aka weeds, for the rest of the days of his life.

I think, though, the worst part of the consequences to their sin was not the pain, sorrow, or laborious work looming before them. I believe God put them outside of the Garden because their sin had caused a separation between them and God. On top of that, God found it necessary to place Cherubim at the east of the Garden of Eden with a flaming sword which turned every way to keep them from touching the tree of life. Adam and Eve were never allowed to enter into the Garden again because of that broken trust between them and God.

Don't you just hate it when a wonderful relationship goes bad? Not to say relationships cannot be mended, because they can. However, a broken relationship will remain that way unless the wrongdoer takes responsibility for his actions, confesses with a repentant heart, and asks for forgiveness. One's pride will hinder the repairing of a broken relationship because the wrongdoer refuses to acknowledge he is wrong and is unwilling to ask for forgiveness from the others involved in the relationship.

Adam and Eve's sin created a need; the blood of an innocent animal had to be shed to make an appropriate covering for them. The LORD God made coats from the animal skins to clothe Adam and Eve properly. That sinful moment spent satisfying their lustful desire by eating of the forbidden fruit had cost them plenty: the tranquility and ease of their lovely home, plus it must have been horrifying for them to watch that innocent animal (most likely one of their pets) die because of their sinful actions, not to mention how everything had affected their relationship with God.

That poor innocent animal's death is a picture of what was to come, the death of Christ on the Cross at Calvary. You see, *"For all have sinned, and come short of the glory of God." (Romans 3:23)* You see, *"For the wages of sin is death...." (Romans 6:23)* So the animal had to be sacrificed because of Adam and Eve's sin, and Christ would be sacrificed because of the sins of the world. *"Then when lust hath conceived, it bringeth forth sin: and sin, when it is finished, bringeth forth death."(James 1:15)*

Chapter 2

Pride

Webster's Elementary Dictionary for Boys and Girls definition of *pride* as a noun: "the condition or fact of being proud." "an unreasonably high opinion of one's own beauty, wealth, etc.; conceit." "self-respect; a proper favorable feeling about one's own position, deeds, etc...." "anything of which a person is proud." "proud or haughty behavior; disdain."– as a verb: "to be proud of something; as, he prides himself on his skill."

Pride, the sin of all sins in my opinion, that self-important and arrogant show of superiority, is devastating to say the least. When combined with egotistical conceit and insensitivity toward others, it can only be described as horrifying. Pride and vanity go hand in hand. I was truly shocked when I looked up the word *vain*. Maybe you will be too. So hold on, the definitions get pretty rough. As stated in the *Webster's Elementary Dictionary for Boys and Girls: vain* as an adjective means "without real worth or value; empty, worthless," "without success; futile," "proud, conceited." *Vanity*, as a noun means the same except "excessive pride" was at the top of the list. The synonym *futile* emphasizes empty of significance. So in a nut shell, *pride* and *vanity* mean "without worth or value, unsuccessful, and *empty of significance*." WOW!

Pride is all about one's self, the benefits gained by any means, no matter the cost or at whose expense. It's all about the pats on the back by one and all, and let's not forget the "look at me go now" attitude, including the body language that accompanies that whole act. Then there is that self-knowing projection of "I'm all that and then some" constantly being shoved in your face, just in case you might forget "just how wonderful I really am." Then as a relentless reminder, they reword the same sentence with, "Wow! I am just too fabulous for words, aren't I?" Pride is a hideous sin, don't you think?

Now, in most cases the prideful one is not quite that obvious, but I believe I have painted a pretty accurate picture of PRIDE. A prideful person is so hard to be around, and honestly, it is one of those sins that can beset any one of us, at any one given moment, and without warning I might add. So we need to be kind. Don't get me wrong. We do not have to tolerate the arrogance of the proud one, but I dare say they will not take the news well when we tell them the truth after they have asked what we think about any situation they are dealing with.

We really do need to remember, "But for the grace of God, there go I–again." Keeping in mind, the truth will make them free, so they do need to hear the truth but only if they ask. It just may be that after you tell them the truth, they will set you free, but only after you have suffered their wrath. There are consequences to be paid when you point your finger in the direction of their haughtiness. Vengeance is on the way.

Actually the Bible has a lot to say about pride, and none of it is good. God certainly is not happy with pride–that is for sure. *Proverbs 6:16-19* says, *"These six things doth the LORD hate: yea, seven are an abomination unto him: A proud look, a lying tongue, and hands that shed innocent blood, An heart that deviseth wicked imaginations, feet that be swift in running to mischief, A false witness that speaketh lies, and he that soweth discord among brethren."*

If I read that particular Scripture correctly, pride is an abomination to God. In other words, He **intensely dislikes** pride; it is something horrible and shameful to Him, not to mention the total disrespect involved when a person is steeped in pride. But notice it said *"a proud look,"* so just a smug look is an abomination to Him. Can you imagine what God thinks of the actions that follow that smug look? He is not fond of *"a false witness that speaketh lies,"* either. The prideful person will be forced to tell many lies because the gig would be up otherwise. So, you can add *"a lying tongue"* and *"he that soweth discord among brethren"* to the growing list of abominations. That part about *"hands that shed innocent blood"* comes later but not before *"an heart that deviseth wicked imaginations"* or *"feet that be swift in running to mischief."* Pride will take you down a horrifying path of destruction. Many will be wounded, if not destroyed, along the way, which of course includes the prideful one.

Some folks do not recognize they are being prideful. It has always amazed me that the ones full of pride are never wrong in their opinions; neither do they want to be confronted or held accountable and are usually on the defense without reason. I am going to hang by a thread here and say that prideful people are very insecure is the reason they find it necessary for all attention to be focused on them. The driving need for all things to go their way and the desire to always be right show how important they think they are. It is all about having the power of control, and they hone their skills and soon become masters of manipulation.

I've also noticed that some insecure folks are very mean and have malice in their heart. They have a wish to do harm; in fact, they intend to hurt you in any way they can: emotionally, physically, and spiritually, if possible. The prideful one is trying to make his victims look worse than he is feeling. Of course, if the prideful one is exposed or caught in the act of cruelty, he is publicly very apologetic but has absolutely no remorse. Prideful ones think they have convinced everyone, including themselves and their wounded victims, there was no malice involved or intended, but it is way too obvious that they are not the least bit sorry for their actions or motives. They are just sorry they got caught.

Meanwhile, just outside the Garden of Eden, in the now sin cursed world, (thanks to Adam and Eve), weeds are growing out of control, and Eve has experienced the sorrow of bringing forth children. Her firstborn son Cain has murdered his brother Abel, all due to the sins of pride and jealousy.

Cain was a tiller of the ground, and Abel was a keeper of the sheep. In other words, Cain worked in his garden plowing, planting, weeding, and pruning until it was time to harvest his crops, while Abel fed the sheep. Then when it was time to sacrifice unto the Lord, Cain brought the fruit of the ground as his offering, while Abel brought the firstlings of his flock. The Lord had respect for Abel's offering but not for Cain's, and the Bible says, *"...Cain was very wroth, and his countenance fell...." (Genesis 4:5)* So because God had rejected Cain's offering, Cain got mad at God but blamed his brother Abel for God's rejecting the offering Cain had worked so hard for. *Wroth* means "extremely angry" and *countenance* means "a facial expression and or composure." Cain thought all of his hard work should have earned him God's respect. I guess Cain didn't know it wasn't about his works but was all about the shed blood of the innocent lamb. The lamb Abel sacrificed that day was the representation of the shed blood of the Lamb of God, Jesus Christ. The acknowledgment and acceptance of the death of Jesus on the cross at Calvary is the only way to have our sins forgiven. *John 14:6* says, *"Jesus saith unto him, I am the way, the truth, and the life: no man cometh unto the Father, but by me."* And *Ephesians 2:8, 9*, says, *"For by grace are ye saved through faith; and that not of yourselves: it is the gift of God: Not of works, lest any man should boast."*

As pride and vanity progress, jealousy isn't far behind, creating anxiety and anger. This progression quickly turns to hatred and revenge. ***Proverbs 13:10*** says*, "Only by pride cometh contention: but with the well advised is wisdom."* There is nothing good about sin and the many plagues that will follow. No matter how hard one tries to hide them, they are still very obvious for the outsider to see.

My pride has gotten me into trouble so many times and has kept me there until I was ready to humble myself or be humbled by my action's being exposed at the most inopportune times. I am sad to say, the humbling did not occur before many of those situations spiraled so far out of control there was no honorable way of escape. That is when the consequences began to trickle and then pour into my life, which only made matters worse than I could ever have imagined.

I have lived with the sins of pride, vanity and jealousy as the giver and as the receiver, and I hated every minute of it. I wish I would have avoided these sins at all costs; they were just the beginning of a downward slippery slope. Lying soon became a way of life out of fear of being exposed and of losing my gained power and control over others. One must keep in mind that whenever pride is involved, shame follows shortly thereafter. That, of course, was confirmed when I read ***Proverbs 11:2, "When pride cometh, then cometh shame: but with the lowly is wisdom."*** *Lowly* as an adjective means "meek, simple and modest in character, also a humble way of behaving." *Wisdom* as a noun means "having good sense, the ability to make sensible and wise decisions; accumulated learning and knowledge gained through experience."

As the sins of pride, vanity and jealousy go unchecked, coveting will progressively gain ground in your life. Coveting is the desire for more, bigger and better than those around you have already acquired. I can tell you that covetousness opens up yet another door to self destruction. Greed and materialism soon join the growing list of sins, and they just fan the flames of pride, jealousy, and vanity. Coveting will supersede whatever good sense you had, rendering you a slave to obtaining that person, place, or thing desired, using any means necessary. When you realize coveting has crept into your life, stop! Regain gratefulness for what you already have, or without fail, covetousness and the accompanying progression of unchecked sin will be your downfall.

A prideful person does not seek God. After all, why should he while in his pride he feels he is capable of doing just fine on his own. As a matter of fact, the prideful one does not even acknowledge or fear God. The Bible says in *1 John 2:16, "For all that is in the world, the lust of the flesh, and the lust of the eyes, and the pride of life, is not of the Father, but is of the world." Psalms 10:4* says, *"The wicked, through the pride of his countenance, will not seek after God: God is not in all his thoughts."* Wicked, YIKES! Who wants to be known as wicked? *Wicked* means "morally bad, sinful, vile, horrid and roguish." When I looked up *roguish,* I cringed because as an adjective it means "malicious," and *malicious* as an adjective means "hateful, spiteful, mean, nasty and cruel." Now I do not have to tell you that this list of adjectives is not attractive on anyone, but to have them linked to someone who claims to be a Christian…? How dishonoring to God, yet glorifying to Satan. But then that is Satan's main objective, to lure one into the false idea that he is good enough on his own without the need for God.

Proverbs 14:3a says, *"In the mouth of the foolish is a rod of pride*…." Oh no, not foolish too! I cannot even bear to put the meaning of *foolish* on paper; the definition included things like "stupid" and "idiotic," not to mention "unimportant" and "unwise." It is just too painful to go on with this definition. The word *foolish* and the meaning of it bring back way too many distasteful memories from my life years ago.

Proverbs 8:13 says, *"The fear of the LORD is to hate evil: pride, and arrogancy, and the evil way, and the froward*

21

mouth, do I hate." Wow! And now we can add *froward* to the list of adjectives concerning pride. *Froward* means "stubbornly disobedient or contrary, difficult to deal with." OH, YIKES! Stubbornly disobedient, that was me!

We are to hate evil, pride, arrogance, and the evil way, along with the forward mouth, as much as the LORD, but how? *Psalms 119:9* says, *"Wherewithal shall a young man cleanse his way? by taking heed thereto according to thy word."* So, reading the Bible, which is the Word of God, is what will cleanse your ways. In *Psalms 119:11* the Psalmist said, *"Thy word have I hid in mine heart, that I might not sin against thee."* Memorizing Scripture will be very helpful in keeping you reminded of those things the LORD hates.

Chapter 3

Jealousy

Webster's Elementary Dictionary for Boys and Girls definition of *jealous*, adj.: "demanding complete devotion; as, a jealous God." "fearful or suspicious of a rival or competitor; feeling a spiteful envy toward someone more successful than oneself." "suspicious that a person one loves is not faithful." "watchful; careful; as, jealous of one's own health."

My sisters accused me of being Mom's favorite. For years I did not understand why my sisters called me names and wouldn't let me play with them unless they were made to. Siblings can be cruel when they think there is favoritism living in the home. Jealousy and envy take a front row seat with them, and the trouble begins.

We have all experienced jealousy at one time or another and probably have been on both the giving and receiving ends of this gross sin. I use the word *gross* because of its definition; *gross* means "overall obviously wrong and not only disgusting, but vulgar; without good taste." If that is not descriptive enough to make you sit up and take notice, then to finalize the thought, I will add that *jealousy* means "awful, uncivilized and dreadfully uncouth." Now the word *uncouth* should extinguish all thoughts of jealousy once and for all because it means "impolite, rude, foul-mouthed and crude." The person on the giving end of jealousy is in the most dangerous position; however, the receiver is going to have a hard time of it also.

As an adult and having raised children of my own, I can see where my sisters may have felt left out. I was a sick child, and my crying must have driven my poor mother right out of her mind. She carried me around and catered to my every whimper, and I am sure it was just to keep the crying to a minimum and for no other reason. It did not help at all when on my worst days I did not want her out of my sight, so when the crying began, she would instantly reappear. Let's see, I could have been called "spoiled" or "an intolerable brat" but certainly not "the favorite." *Favorite* as a noun means "a person or a thing that is favored above others." As an adjective it means "favored; preferred; best-liked." So the question is, was I the favorite or just a spoiled brat?

Favoritism in a family should be avoided because it provokes and promotes jealousy. There are several examples of favoritism in the Bible, and they all have an unfavorable ending. For instance, Isaac and Rebekah had the first set of twins, Esau and Jacob. ***Genesis 25:28*** says, ***"And Isaac loved Esau… but Rebekah loved Jacob."*** Talk about your dysfunctional family–when Rebekah overheard a conversation between Isaac and Esau, she sprang into action. She thought up a plan to trick her husband into thinking her beloved Jacob was Esau so Jacob would receive the blessing from their father instead of Esau the firstborn. Rebekah's deceptive plan worked too, but what a path of destruction and near death her idea turned out to be. ***Genesis 27:41a*** says, ***"And Esau hated Jacob because of the blessing wherewith his father blessed him…."*** Instead of Esau's blaming his mother, whose deceptive plan it was to deprive him of his birthright, Esau **hated** and blamed his brother *"…and Esau said in his heart, The days of mourning for my father are at hand; then will I slay my brother Jacob."(Genesis 27:41b)*

Thoughts, if not the actual act, of murder can follow closely behind the sins of pride and jealousy when hatred, bitterness and revenge are allowed to enter into one's heart. Here in *Genesis 27:42b* are the words of warning Rebekah spoke to Jacob, *"...Behold, thy brother Esau, as touching thee, doth comfort himself, purposing to kill thee."* Esau had told his mother of his plan to kill his brother and would have carried out his plan of murder, but she intervened. Rebekah warned Jacob of Esau's intentions and told Jacob to leave, to go to her brother Laban's house, and to stay there until Esau's **fury** had subsided, giving him time to forget what had happened.

First of all, may I say in my own life I have never forgotten any of the events where deception was involved without forgiving the offender first? I can honestly say there are a few occurrences I may never forget, even though I have forgiven the offences. I firmly believe forgiving those who have wronged you is a must for your sake if for no other reason than for your peace of mind. Your unforgiving spirit always grieves the Holy Spirit, and you are in danger of becoming just as angry and bitter as the one who wronged you, and I would like to add, we do not have to forgive the sin, only the sinner. Now if you have never accepted Christ as your personal Savior, then you may not truly understand the peace of true forgiveness.

Jealousy is a mean, vicious, destructive and sinful way of life. The sin of jealousy places you in bondage, renders you useless and out of control, and will consume your every thought. As a matter of fact, jealousy can lead to murder! Yes, I said murder! Now you may not actually kill someone with your hands, but you can kill them in your heart by wishing that person dead and out of your life. You will go out of your way to say hateful things just to hurt them. If you give way to jealousy, soon you will be living a life of deceit, and when confronted, deceitfulness will lead to denial with one lie following right after another. Well, what kind of life is that? It is a life of suspicious rivalry, spiteful envy, anger and resentment. This condition only gets worse as time goes on; bitterness and rage will soon enter into the situation. Jealousy comes from the heart and can only be described as ungratefulness. People that have an ungrateful heart have no respect for God or any authority for that matter.

Maybe your situation is the feeling of being left out or over-looked. Perhaps you feel you are not being treated fairly or not accepted for who you are. Or are you frustrated because you are not the one in control? A person plagued with jealousy is a person on a mission. Most of the time that person is seeking importance and to be elevated to the position of always being in control. Jealous people hope to gain a better feeling about themselves. In reality, jealousy is the ultimate act of selfishness. A person with a jealousy problem has a deadly problem, and unless the problem is dealt with, that person will never obtain a peaceful life. Jealousy starts at a very early age, is extremely sensitive and easily provoked, so any signs of favoritism only fan the flames of jealousy.

People are people, and none of us are without sin. Sin comes so naturally to us; in fact, it is our very nature, and we are drawn to the sinful things of this world. The people in the Bible are not just some made-up characters in a story, compiled and located in a book called the Bible. They were real people and had the same daily concerns we have today; remember, there is nothing new under the sun.

Go ahead, take a deep breath and keep reading because there is good news on the way. We can take advantage of the history given to us through the Bible. We can read about the examples of those people who have already lived their lives and see the different ways jealousy has affected so many folks from one generation to another. We can overcome jealousy before it gets a grip on us–yes, before jealousy advances to envy, greed, resentment, anger, and hatred brought on by one individual's selfishness and desire for control. We can overcome jealousy before the root of bitterness has the chance to take hold, thus preventing the destruction all those emotions will bring into so many lives.

If you know the story of Joseph, then you know he was the favorite son of his father Jacob, aka Israel. Remember, God changed Jacob's name. *"And he said, Thy name shall be called no more Jacob, but Israel…." (Genesis 32:28)* Jacob married sisters, Leah and Rachel. He loved Rachel and worked seven years for his Uncle Laban, Rachel's father, to receive her hand in marriage, but through deception and selfish motives, Jacob was given Leah instead. Well, how rude was that?

At first you might think that was a terrible trick to pull on a young man. I mean, come on. Can't you just see it now: the two little lovebirds have stared longingly into each other's eyes for seven years, thinking they might just die before they hear the sound of wedding bells ringing throughout the land? And then old Uncle Laban pulls this lousy, lowdown trick by slipping his tender eyed oldest daughter Leah in the place of Jacob's lovely Rachel.

Well, before we get all judgmental, let's not forget a few things: Laban and Rebekah, Jacob's mother, were brother and sister; I think they lived in a household where deception was a common way of life for them. Rebekah was a deceiver and showed her children the way to that path when she convinced Jacob to deceive his father in that birthright blessing ordeal. Sir Walter Scott said it best with, "Oh what a tangled web we weave, when first we practice to deceive." I have a feeling this was not Rebekah's first lesson of deception either; I think it was a part of her daily dealings. We only know what we are taught. I believe Albert Schweitzer was correct when he wrote, "Example is not the main thing in influencing others. It's the only thing." So when we casually live with our sin, it becomes causality to those around us, and it is not surprising when we see the same sins appear in families from one generation to another, like it says in the fourth of the ten commandments, *Exodus 20:5, "…visiting the iniquity of the fathers upon the children unto the third and fourth generation of them that hate me."* So don't forget, whatever you plant in your life's garden is what you will eventually harvest. The Bible says in *Job 4:8, "…they that plow iniquity, and sow wickedness, reap the same."* Another principle in the Bible on this subject is found in *Hosea 8:7, "For they have sown the wind, and they shall reap the whirlwind…."* In this case deceitfulness produced more of the same.

After working another seven years for his Uncle Laban, Jacob finally received his beloved Rachel as his wife. *"…And he loved also Rachel more than Leah…." (Genesis 29:30)* Isn't that special? I can hear it now, can't you? "Oh, yoo-hoo, uh, Leah, the one I really love is here now, so if you don't mind, I'll see you later. Gotta go now. Bye, bye."

I am sure the ugly green-eyed monster of jealousy, along with its relative, envy, kept Leah's tears flowing until the freshness of the reality of Jacob and Rachel's marriage had some time to settle in. Leah must have been brokenhearted as Jacob spent less time with her so he could spend more time with his favorite wife, her beautiful and favored sister Rachel.

The Bible says in *Genesis 29:17, "Leah was tender eyed; but Rachel was beautiful and well favoured."* It has been said, "Beauty is in the eye of the beholder" and "Beauty is as beauty does," but the truth is *"Favour is deceitful, and beauty is vain: but a woman that feareth the LORD, she shall be praised." (Proverbs 31:30)* Leah was not only tender eyed; I believe she was tender hearted also. She was the total opposite of her beautiful and well favoured sister Rachel who truly had their husband Jacob's heart. I do not think Leah was bitter or angry, but brokenhearted, and I have no doubt she knew all along she was not Jacob's first choice as his wife.

I have a feeling Rachel did not keep her jealousy toward Leah a secret. *"And when the LORD saw that Leah was hated, he opened her womb…." (Genesis 29:31a)* Hated? Who in the world could have possibly hated tender eyed Leah?

Why, her beautiful sister Rachel of course. But what would Rachel have to be jealous of Leah about? She had it all–looks, anything she wanted, and their husband's full attention, *"… but Rachel was barren." (Genesis 29:31b)* Back in that era it was the worst if you did not have sons, but no children at all, YIKES! Notice the Scripture says, *"…the LORD saw that Leah was hated…"* so the opening and shutting of the womb was the LORD'S work, but because of Rachel's inability to have children, she **hated** Leah instead of the LORD.

You know there were jealousy problems in this family because of favoritism. The children could not help but notice how differently their father treated his two wives and their two handmaids which Jacob also had sons with. The real trouble began when his favorite wife Rachel gave birth to the long-awaited and favorite son Joseph. It wasn't long before jealousy turned to **hatred** and progressed to thoughts of murder by the ten older brothers. *"Now Israel loved Joseph more than all his children, because he was the son of his old age: and he made him a coat of many colours. And when his brethren saw that their father loved him more than all his brethren, they hated him, and could not speak peaceably unto him." (Genesis 37:3, 4)*

Jacob's family was no different than the families of today, where multiple husbands and/or wives are involved and things really get out of control when there are children from each of those different relationships, more commonly called the blended family of yours, mine, and ours.

In this case Jacob was the only father of all the children the four different women gave birth to, and you can see the jealousy coming from every direction. Not one of them felt the love and security they wanted and needed from Jacob, not even the wives. Way back in Genesis, God's plan was for the family to be made of one man and one woman. The two of them became one in marriage. *Genesis 2:24* says, *"Therefore shall a man leave his father and his mother, and shall cleave unto his wife: and they shall be one flesh."* But when sin entered into the lives of Adam and Eve, it entered into the family also. You can tell by the following scripture found in *Mathew 19:6* that God had no intentions of the family's splitting up: *"Wherefore they are no more twain, but one flesh. What therefore God hath joined together, let not man put asunder."*

Chapter 4

Selfishness

Webster's Elementary Dictionary for Boys and Girls definition of *selfish*, adj.; "caring too much for one's own interests, advancement, etc.; as, a *selfish* child; also, having to do with a person who thinks too much of securing or advancing his own personal interests; as, *selfish* pleasure."

In most cases insecurity is the cause of jealousy. Jealousy and selfishness also go hand in hand; they create anxiety, anger, fear, and loneliness. There is nothing attractive or lovely about a selfish person, no matter how physically attractive that person is. ***Proverbs 22:1*** tells us, ***"A good name is rather to be chosen than great riches, and loving favour rather than silver and gold."*** Our reputation will beat us to our destination. ***Proverbs 20:11*** says, ***"Even a child is known by his doings, whether his work be pure, and whether it be right."***

Selfish people are actually repulsive to others, are never kind, and will soon expose their envy, which they hope has been hidden from public view. Selfish, selfishness, self-centeredness all pretty much mean the same thing and point to one's self. You don't have to know a person very long to recognize if he is a selfish individual. Self-centeredness is usually very obvious and can be detected almost immediately through casual conversation or by interaction. The conversation will be all about that person, and if by chance the topic is changed or interrupted, he will always bring it back to himself. A selfish person is full of pride, and strife begins when things do not go his way. Self-centeredness is insensitive and lacks consideration for others, even if they are people the selfish one claims to love very much. Because of their preoccupation and pursuit of their own satisfaction, selfish people do not care who has to be stepped on, discredited, or destroyed in the process of reaching their self-centered goal.

I cannot help but think about the two children that were sent to play in a room full of toys. One child was extremely selfish to the point that he would grab away every toy the other child picked up, saying, "I want to play with that one." With so many other toys to choose from, the other child would simply pick another toy, but each time the selfish child would grab the toy from him, claiming **that** was the one he was going to pick. This went on until the selfish child had every toy stashed in a corner or so tightly held in his grip that he could not play with a single one of them. Consequently, the selfish child was in bondage guarding his ill-gotten loot, while the other child was free to move about the room, happily entertaining himself without the need for one single toy.

Now don't get me wrong. We are all selfish in some form or fashion, but we do not have to live our lives with selfish thoughts or motives dictating our every move. We will be remembered by our dominate characteristics, good or bad.

By now you have probably noticed you cannot have just one sin in your life. Sin is like a roaring fire and can get out of control just as fast. One sin leads to another until it is ruling your every motive and move. The sins of jealousy and selfishness are no different. The Bible says in *Genesis 37:4* that Joseph's brothers hated him so much they could not even speak peaceably to him. *"And when his brethren saw that their father loved him more than all his brethren, they hated him, and could not speak peaceably unto him."* When I was growing up, I was told that if I hated someone, it meant I would rather see them dead. Yikes, that sounds pretty harsh, doesn't it? *Hate* is a very strong word which means "to dislike intensely." Can you imagine the disharmony that went on in this obviously dysfunctional family?

I never allowed my boys to speak rudely or unkindly to each other, nor were they allowed to fight beyond a slight disagreement. When they were growing up, I let them work things out between themselves for the most part, but if a disagreement turned into an argument, I stepped in as the mediator. Once the details were given and settled, my work was done. However, if there were anymore outbursts that same day involving the disgruntled little trouble-seekers, they had to sit with their arms around each other in a corner facing the wall. Soon I would hear them whispering, quietly laughing, and having a good time. That was the signal that all had been forgiven between them, and I let them out of the corner, but not before they were made to give each other a hug and a kiss. This is how I handled all arguments until the age of eleven or twelve, when they refused to kiss each other, so we moved on to the more mature method of handshaking instead. Only a few times I had to resort to a more drastic punishment, but I did whatever was necessary to smooth out anger before it had the chance to give way to resentment, bitterness, or revenge.

Joseph's brothers' intense hostility was caused by pride, jealousy, hatred, and began to include envy. *Genesis 37:11 says, "...And his brethren envied him...."* Their anger had been raging for so long there was no rational thinking, self-control or self-discipline involved. It did not help matters any at all when Joseph had a few dreams and shared them with his family, telling them they would all be bowing down to him one day. Are you kidding me? Joseph's outrageous statements just intensified his brothers' hatred towards him.

Then one day Joseph was sent to Shechem where his ten older brothers were tending Jacob's sheep. Their father Jacob wanted Joseph to find his brothers and return with a full report as to how things were going. Now you know the brothers only saw this as a tattletale event, even though Joseph was simply following their father's request. I have no doubt Joseph had developed a snooty attitude towards his brothers over the years caused by the different kinds of mistreatment he had received from each of them. Joseph was allowed to get away with so many things they were not allow to get away with, including his "tone and 'tude," which only kept the fiery flames of fury stirred up within his brothers.

When Joseph's brothers saw him coming across the field, they said something like this, "Oh, look. Here comes the little dreamer now." The plot thickens in *Genesis 37:18, "And when they saw him afar off, even before he came near unto them, they conspired against him to slay him."* *Slay* means "to put to death with a weapon or by violence, to kill." *Conspire* means "secretly plan to act illegally" or "to work together." Well, that just sounds like premeditated murder to me. What do you think?

The brothers hated Joseph and his coat of many colors that their father had made and given to him. The coat was just another reminder of Joseph's elevated position compared to theirs; and now those ridiculous dreams declaring they would be bowing down to him one day were more than they could deal with. Who did he think he was anyway? Well, if they killed him and threw him in a pit somewhere, there would be no bowing down to the smug little brat, now would there? Yes indeedy, they all thought this would be the solution to all their problems, so *Genesis 37:20* tells us that they decided how they would explain Joseph's disappearance to their father: *"...we will say, some evil beast hath devoured him...."*

The brothers fully intended to kill Joseph, but the thought of a physical murder was too much for the oldest brother

Reuben, so Reuben told them, *"...Shed no blood, but cast him into this pit that is in the wilderness, and lay no hand upon him;"* Reuben's intentions were *"that he might rid him out of their hands, to deliver him to his father again." (Genesis 37:22)* When Joseph finally walked into the camp where his brothers were, they stripped him of his coat of many colors and threw him in a pit without water. Without water Joseph would surely have died by the thoughts and intents of his brothers hearts and not by their hands.

Murder is murder no matter the method. The intents of the mind and heart are in many aspects equal to murder by the hand. The jealous one still wishes his rival literally dead and out of his life. Joseph's brothers thought all their problems would be solved if Joseph was no longer amongst the living; you might just be thinking the same about your situation. Well Joseph was not the problem. You see, Joseph's brothers thought too highly of themselves. Their real problem was ungratefulness. They thought they deserved more than they were receiving, and when their expectations were not met, they were disappointed. They most likely felt cheated, unnoticed, and unloved.

When a person is not content with what he has or how he is being treated by others, he will develop an ungrateful spirit; he will believe the old saying, "The grass is always greener on the other side of the fence," and the pity party begins.

I am not saying Joseph's brothers did not have legitimate needs and desires that were not being met or that they did not have justifiable complaints because I believe they did. But look at what happened. They blamed and held Joseph responsible for their lack when their father Jacob was truly the one to blame, **if** there was even blame to be given.

Remember in *Genesis 37:3a* the Bible says, *"Now Israel loved Joseph more than all his children, because he was the son of his old age...."* Was Israel (Jacob) wrong for loving Joseph more than his other children? That is not for me to say; however, it did affect Joseph's life in a negative way also. The extra indulgences afforded Joseph by his father angered Joseph's brothers and most likely created a sense of arrogance in Joseph, which intensified their hatred towards him. When all those emotions were not dealt with in the proper manner, things just went from bad to worse–well, to the thoughts of murder is where those emotions led. In *Ecclesiastes 7:9b* the Bible says, *"...for anger resteth in the bosom of fools."* And in *Jeremiah 17:9* the Bible says, *"The heart is deceitful above all things, and desperately wicked: who can know it?"*

The Bible clearly states in *Colossians 3:21, "Fathers, provoke not your children to anger, lest they be discouraged."* Joseph's brothers were discouraged without a doubt. You can bet the rest of the family was discouraged also, although for different reasons. Disharmony is very contagious and spreads quickly. *Proverbs 27:4* says, *"Wrath is cruel, and anger is outrageous; but who is able to stand before envy?"*

Looking back in my own life, when I got away with things my sisters would be in trouble for doing, my courage to continue pushing the limits in the wrong direction grew, and nothing but trouble came from it. I remember when my sisters were mean to me or wouldn't let me play, I resented them for it. So in retaliation I would tattletale on them because I knew they would be in trouble, which only made them hate me even more.

Envy is very difficult to cope with. One of my sisters admitted wanting nothing to do with me for years because envy had placed a wedge in our relationship. Envy changed into resentment little by little, day after day, and year after year through the frustration caused by her own feelings over not receiving the same amount of attention from our mother as I did. Due to the lack of communication and explanation, the frustration developed into anger and bitterness, with violence always at the edge of her defense.

Meanwhile Joseph was sitting it out in the pit as his brothers were eating their dinner when they saw in the distance a company of Ishmaelites coming their way. Judah, the fourth born son to tender-eyed Leah, came up with the lucrative idea; if we can't kill Joseph to get him out of our way, let's sell him for twenty pieces of silver, *"…for he is our brother and our flesh…." (Genesis 37:27)* Everyone there agreed, and Joseph was out of the pit and on the road to Egypt.

Don't you find it strange that Reuben walked away knowing his other brothers were more than willing to murder Joseph? Reuben fully intended to make sure Joseph, "the arrogant little brat," was safely returned home to their father, and Rueben temporarily soothed his conscience by suggesting they put Joseph in a pit instead of shedding his blood. Reuben wanted to believe that he was doing the right thing, but he would have been just as guilty as the others if they had killed Joseph in his absence. And because he did not take the proper precautions to keep Joseph from the intended harm, I believe Reuben was overwhelmed with guilt when he returned only to find that Joseph was gone–the pit was empty.

In the absence of Rueben the other brothers had sold Joseph into slavery, or so they thought. Now their consciences were not bothering them over the death they had planned, they had gained some extra money, and they had devised the perfect explanation for the disappearance of their father's favorite son. And best of all, he was no longer standing in the way of their receiving the attention they wanted from their father, but as it turns out, nothing could have been further from the truth.

Chapter 5

Bitterness

Webster's Elementary Dictionary for Boys and Girls definition of *bitterness* as a noun: "disagreeable; distasteful; as, bitter insults, painful; arising from anger." From the *Encarta Dictionary* as an adjective: "resentful; difficult to accept; hostile; very cold."

The death of my mother was a devastating reality, and I found no comfort at all knowing my father's cousin had led her to the saving knowledge of Jesus Christ. Though I saw a definite change in her demeanor after she had accepted Christ as her personal Saviour those few hours before she slipped away, I was still skeptical when she told me she was going to Heaven. Out of curiosity I asked her how she knew that for sure, and she said, "Because Jesus told me so." I have since learned that when Jesus says something is **so**, it really is **so**.

I spent years mourning the loss of my mother, wishing I could see her just one more time and knowing I would never have that opportunity. It only made life more difficult to face on a daily basis. Because I knew nothing at all about salvation, her acceptance of Christ meant nothing to me. It was not until I accepted Jesus Christ as my personal Saviour that I realized I would see her again. Her death was no longer a loss to me, knowing we would spend eternity in Heaven together. That knowledge changed my demeanor, and I had a brand new outlook on life and death.

After our mother's death, I consciously and continually made efforts to communicate with the two sisters I did not have any kind of a relationship with at all; they still chose to shut me out. One of those two sisters was the envious and bitter sister who eventually came to the saving knowledge of Jesus Christ also. Through regular church attendance and Bible reading, she was able to recognize how her bitterness, anger, and resentment had held her in bondage for many years. She also found that Christian fellowship and the tutelage of women's Bible studies helped her to recognize that some of the problems in her life had been brought on by herself. Once she was able to get past denial, she was able to acknowledge her sin, and with confession she was able to drop all those unnecessary defenses. Thus her tendencies towards violence were quenched. Then and only then was she able to stop taking even our most causal conversation as a personal affront. This enabled her to actually like me, leaving the door open for us to develop a new and real relationship, not only as sisters but as sisters in Christ. Hallelujah to it all! I am especially excited about those violent tendencies' being quenched. Yikes!

Meanwhile in the story of Joseph's life, Reuben returned to pull Joseph out of the pit and found the pit was empty, *"... he rent his clothes." (Genesis 37:29)* Reuben went straight to his brothers, wanting to know the whereabouts of Joseph. As the oldest son, Reuben knew he would be held responsible for answering all the questions their father would be asking when they arrived home without Joseph in tow.

Judah's idea of selling Joseph for a few pieces of silver now needed an alibi. *"And they took Joseph's coat, and killed a kid of the goats, and dipped the coat in the blood; And they sent the coat of many colours, and they brought it to their father; and said, This have we found: know now whether it be thy son's coat or no." (Genesis 37:31, 32)* Well, well, well, what a devious plan Jacob's ten older sons had in store for him when they handed their father the familiar and bloodstained coat, allowing him to believe it was covered with Joseph's very own blood. Little did Joseph's brothers know that the lies and manipulations, the plotting and planning they had carefully executed in secret would eventually be exposed publicly. And *"…be sure your sin will find you out." (Numbers 32:23)*

God knows **all**, hears **all**, sees **all** and is in control of **all** – at **all** times. Nothing ever gets by God. ***Psalm 139:3, 4,*** says, ***"Thou compassest my path and my lying down, and art acquainted with all my ways. For there is not a word in my tongue, but, lo, O LORD, thou knowest it altogether."***

I am sure the brothers had not anticipated how Judah's idea of faking Joseph's death would affect their father. But no doubt they began to realize what a horrible impact it did have on Jacob when he rent his clothes, and said ***"…For I will go down into the grave unto my son mourning…." (Genesis 37:35)*** Jacob knew immediately that the blood-covered coat was the one he had previously made for his beloved son Joseph; ***"…It is my son's coat; an evil beast hath devoured him; Joseph is without doubt rent in pieces." (Genesis 37:33).***

As Jacob mourned the loss of Joseph, he refused to be comforted by any of his other children. I cannot imagine how Jacob's statement and refusal of comfort must have made his remaining sons and daughters feel. I am sure it was not the warm, fuzzy feeling his older sons had hoped for when they sold Joseph into slavery. Who knew their plan would backfire on them and would cause them more grief than imaginable, and it was a plan that had sounded so good to them at the time too.

The brothers could have come clean right then and there; they could have confessed the truth about everything: their jealousy, resentment, envy and all the deception. They could have said, "Joseph is still alive; yes, we sold him for money just to get rid of him because we hated him for stealing all your time, love, and attention from the rest of us."

But Joseph's brothers were no different than we are today: pride and fear kept them from confessing their sin just like it keeps us from confessing our sin. The lack of courage put Joseph's jealous brothers deeper and deeper into bondage as their list of sins continued to grow. Pride is the foundation on which our sins are built. It is that conceited, self-important position we place ourselves in that sets us on the path to destruction when our plans or desires are not fulfilled.

Bitterness, envy, and anger, or any other sin in our lives, are the strongholds that can only be torn down by confession. Remember it wasn't until my sister acknowledged her envy and bitterness that she was able to lose those pent-up emotions and the defensive anger that flared up every time we spoke. She had to acknowledge the truth, and when she did, she was made free just like the Bible says in *John 8:32b, "…the truth shall make you free."*

So when "Plan A," which was to kill Joseph, failed, they quickly slipped into "Plan B," and they sold him off into slavery. "Plan B," hadn't worked out for them as well as they thought it would, and they were forced into deceiving their father. Can you believe it? The very person they were craving love and attention from was now a victim to all their deception. It is sad to say, but there are those of us who are willing to go through the entire alphabet of "Plans" to manipulate our way through life trying to gain fame and fortune or whatever… in hopes it will be that which is able to remove the unhappiness that is so "just there" every waking moment and in most cases interferes with a restful night's sleep.

So many times we think it is the other person who is causing our problems. We think if we just had this, that, or the next thing, we would then be happy, when in fact it is not the lack of anything at all that is causing our problems. The real problem is our ungratefulness. We do not appreciate what we do have. Instead we focus on those things we wish we had, thinking that if we acquired them, they would make us happy.

The "poor me program" only prepares the perfect setting for bitterness to take root, which brings us to the worst kind of misery–the self-inflicted kind.

Joseph's brothers envied him; they wanted what he had– their father's love; and no matter how hard they tried, they could not obtain it. They were envious, resentful, hostile, and angry, so much so that they were ready to kill their own brother. ***Proverbs 14:10a*** says, ***"The heart knoweth his own bitterness,"*** and ***Proverbs 14:30 says, "A sound heart is the life of the flesh: but envy the rottenness of the bones."*** The brothers were overwhelmed with envy and bitterness.

Chapter 6

Revenge

Webster's Elementary Dictionary for Boys and Girls definition of *revenge* as a verb: "to inflict harm or injury in return for harm or injury." As a noun: "the act of revenging; also, desire to return evil for evil."

Traveling across the desert could not have been easy for Joseph. It most likely was a hot, humid, dirty and very tiring journey. What could be worse than being held captive and forced to go with strangers into unfamiliar territory? Perhaps nothing–except for the brutal knowledge that his brothers had gladly sold him for profit: just to get him out of their lives.

Isn't it amazing how the selfish decisions made by Jacob's older sons drastically changed so many lives? These sons were so focused on satisfying themselves, they did not anticipate all the heartache, sorrow, and pain they would bring to themselves and to the father they loved.

I asked a very sweet friend of mine if she had ever experienced the desire to seek revenge on anyone in her life, and she said, "No, I don't think so." I found that very refreshing because I could not say that about myself. I have sought revenge on a few people in my life, and I am sad to say I was successful in achieving my goal with some of them.

I wonder what made me think my revenge was going to end the misery I was continually receiving. News flash–there will never be satisfaction in getting even with anyone. The Bible says, *"...avenge not yourselves ...Vengeance is mine; I will repay, saith the Lord." (Romans 12:19)*

My attempts at revenge did not bring about the end of the misery like I thought they would. Misery of a different kind entered into my life. Who knew I would worry myself sick wondering when my acts of cruelty would be discovered. Much to my dismay, the cycle of revenge and cruelty continued as the jealous ones honed their skills and sharpened the edge of the misery they intended to afflict upon me when the opportunity arrived.

People often make statements like these, "You make everything look so easy," or "You always get picked," or my personal favorite, "You always come out smelling like a rose." May I say that things are not always what they seem to be on the surface, some things that appear easy are very difficult to obtain, getting picked means extra work, and last but not least, smells don't finalize a single thing.

Roses are beautiful, and **some** do smell fabulous, but that is only the end result in the life of a rose. Let's not forget about the fertilizing, cultivating, and pruning that are involved. Then there are the pests that come along–the aphids and ants, the birds and the bees and the elements of the great outdoors that must be endured. Roses also must face the overwhelming heat from the sun and the freezing cold when it snows, being tossed to and fro in the wind and the beatings that come from the pouring rain that is sometimes accompanied by hail.

When the rosebuds begin to open, the birds and the bees are immediately attracted to them. Do you know what happens when a bird takes flight? Its droppings land on whatever is under it even if it is a rose, and the bees go straight to the center of the rose and suck out what ever sweet nectar they can get.

Finally, when the rose is picked and placed in even the simplest of vases, its amazing beauty and sweet-smelling fragrance will only last a few days, and it will be no more. It is important to remember that the rose acquired its sweet smell through enduring the many difficulties of its short but very beautiful life.

I have a feeling that Joseph's life looked pretty fabulous to his ten older brothers; remember that Joseph stayed home while they worked in the fields tending their father's flocks. But I know from personal experience, unless you have walked a mile in someone's shoes, you have no idea how rough that mile was for that person and vice versa.

Once again the plot thickens for this family...*"And Joseph was brought down to Egypt; and Potiphar, an officer of Pharaoh, captain of the guard, an Egyptian, bought him of the hands of the Ishmeelites, which had brought him down thither. And the LORD was with Joseph, and he was a prosperous man; and he was in the house of his master the Egyptian. And his master saw that the LORD was with him, and that the LORD made all that he did to prosper in his hand."* (Genesis 39:1-3)

Joseph was not a pampered and spoiled brat who sat around demanding that people wait on him. I believe Joseph was taught many things while he was at home with his father. I also believe Joseph's diligence and obedience intensified the envy of his older brothers.

It takes wisdom, knowledge, and the proper training, along with meticulous hard work and self-discipline, to oversee fields and a household the magnitude of Potiphar's estate. Joseph was still a very young man, yet the Bible says Potiphar *"...left all that he had in Joseph's hand; and he knew not ought he had, save the bread which he did eat. And Joseph was a goodly person, and well favoured."* (Genesis 39:6)

Then in *Genesis 39:7* the Bible says Potiphar's wife, *"...cast her eyes upon Joseph; and she said, Lie with me."*

WELL, YIKES! That certainly must have caught Joseph off guard. Joseph refused her sexual advances and said, *"...how then can I do this great wickedness, and sin against God?" (Genesis 39:9)* Because of Joseph's honor, love, and respect for God, he was able to abstain from such wickedness.

In *Psalm 51:4* King David acknowledged that he had sinned against God when he committed adultery with Bathsheba. *"Against thee, thee only, have I sinned, and done this evil in thy sight...."* We have a natural tendency to believe we are sinning against people, but sin is always against God, including the sin of revenge.

Potiphar's wife continued to tempt Joseph day by day, but he refused to fall into her seductive trap. Then one day *"... Joseph went into the house to do his business; and there was none of the men of the house there within. And she caught him by his garment, saying, Lie with me: and he left his garment in her hand, and fled, and got him out." (Genesis 39:11, 12)*

I have no doubt Potiphar's wife thought very highly of herself and felt completely mortified by Joseph's constant rejection of her lustful attempts. Revenge came easy for that wicked wife with Joseph's garment in hand to prove his alleged inappropriate conduct toward her. She cleverly proclaimed her story to the entire household while she waited the return of her husband, and once he heard the news, Joseph found himself in *"...a place where the king's prisoners were bound: and he was there in the prison." (Genesis 39:20)*

Several years ago there was a situation in my life that took me completely by surprise. I could not believe that after working side by side, several times a week, for many years, with a presumed friend of mine that she had taken fiction and with talented manipulation made certain things look factual. I was absolutely devastated over the entire horrendous ordeal. It was so painful that I actually felt like I had had open heart surgery without anesthesia.

I have no words to describe how difficult that experience was for me, and the only way I was able to get through the suffering was to remind myself that God saw it all, heard it all, and allowed it all to happen. I wiped tears away daily reminding myself that this was a growing experience, a time of pruning to make room for new growth and this too would pass. After all, I had asked God to make me who I needed to be to glorify Him, and this experience was a part of making me who I needed to be.

I find it very interesting that from the time Joseph entered into Egypt, the LORD was with Joseph and made everything he did to prosper, even in prison. *"And the keeper of the prison committed to Joseph's hand all the prisoners that were in the prison; and whatsoever they did there, he was the doer of it. The keeper of the prison looked not to any thing that was under his hand; because the LORD was with him, and that which he did, the LORD made it to prosper." (Genesis 39:22, 23)*

The Bible does not say how the King of Egypt's chief butler and chief baker managed to offend him, but they did, and the King cast them both into prison, *"And the captain of the guard charged Joseph with them, and he served them: and they continued a season in ward." (Genesis 40:4)*

I am a firm believer that God sends certain people into our lives for specific reasons. God knew spiritual growth was not going to be easy for His children. However, spiritual growth is still expected from His children no matter their location or circumstances, even though some of those circumstances may seem impossible for them to get through. The Bible clearly states, *"... with God all things are possible." (Matthew 19:26)*

"I can do all things through Christ which strengtheneth me." (Philippians 4:13) "But thanks be to God, which giveth us the victory through our Lord Jesus Christ." (1 Corinthians 15:57)

One morning after a troubled night of dreams for both the baker and butler, Joseph noticed they were sad, and he asked them what was wrong, *"And they said unto him, We have dreamed a dream, and there is no interpreter of it. And Joseph said unto them, Do not interpretations belong to God? tell me them, I pray you." (Genesis 40:8)* They both told Joseph their dreams and while giving all the credit to God, Joseph interpreted the butler's dream first, *"... The three branches are three days: Yet within three days shall Pharaoh lift up thine head, and restore thee unto thy place... after the former manner when thou wast his butler." (Genesis 40:12, 13)* And just before the conversation ended between the two of them, Joseph said to the butler, *"... make mention of me unto Pharaoh, and bring me out of this house: For indeed I was stolen away out of the land of the Hebrews: and here also have I done nothing that they should put me into the dungeon." (Genesis 40:14, 15)*

Then after hearing the baker's dream, Joseph said, *"...The three baskets are three days ... Yet within three days shall Pharaoh lift up thy head from off thee, and shall hang thee on a tree; and the birds shall eat thy flesh from off thee." (Genesis 40:18, 19)*

Joseph's interpretations were correct: the baker was hanged and the birds did eat his flesh, and the butler was restored to his former position, *"Yet did not the chief butler remember Joseph, but forgat him." (Genesis 40:23)* Isn't that special, Joseph was forgotten by the butler. I just hate it when it happens like that, don't you?

I dare say we have all had to endure false accusation and in defending our self looked like the guilty one. While lacking in character and courage to stand for what was right, our accusers stood back to watch us take the blame. Innocent, yet being held accountable for someone else's actions, we experience the feelings of unfairness. Our emotions quickly advance to anger, then to bitterness, and if left unchecked, those emotions advance even farther to an overwhelming desire to seek revenge as soon as possible.

But friends, if we allow those feeling to take hold, we will be lowering ourselves to the same ungodly level as our accuser. YIKES! Instead we are to, *"...Be careful for nothing; but in every thing by prayer and supplication with thanksgiving let your requests be made known unto God. And the peace of God, which passeth all understanding, shall keep your hearts and minds through Christ Jesus." (Philippians 4:6, 7)* Remember what the Bible says in *Proverbs 16:7 "When a man's ways please the LORD, he maketh even his enemies to be at peace with him*." Now you may need to brace yourself for this one. Are you ready? Okay, *"If thine enemy be hungry, give him bread to eat; and if he be thirsty, give him water to drink: For thou shalt heap coals of fire upon his head, and the LORD shall reward thee." (Proverbs 25:21, 22)*

I do not think Joseph experienced any animosity toward the butler, because Joseph took comfort in knowing God was with him. Although I have no doubt that Joseph was sad and lonely (after all, family is family, even though some of the members were wretched and mistreated him in the worst of ways), I still believe Joseph loved and missed them all.

So who knew that the King of Egypt was going to dream two dreams and that Joseph's flawless reputation of interpreting dreams would be the very thing that got him out of prison and placed second in command of all the land in Egypt by the King himself.

Isn't it amazing how God used all those unscrupulous and sometimes ruthless, heart- breaking situations to groom Joseph for the future? God's very own word tells us, *"...that all things work together for good to them that love God, to them who are the called according to his purpose." (Romans 8:28)*

Being second in command of Egypt was no sit-down, kick-up-your-feet-and-relax job. Joseph went to work, and in the seven years of plenty *"...Joseph gathered corn as the sand of the sea, very much, until he left numbering; for it was without number." (Genesis 41:49)* The famine followed just like Joseph said it would, *"And all countries came into Egypt to Joseph for to buy corn; because that the famine was so sore in all lands." (Genesis 41:57)*

Meanwhile back in the land of Canaan where Jacob and his family dwelled and upon hearing Egypt had corn to sell, Jacob sent his ten oldest sons to Egypt with money in their pockets. Joseph's brothers came to purchase corn for their families, *"...and bowed down themselves before him with their faces to the earth." (Genesis 42:6)* I don't want to sound snooty, but the dream Joseph had shared with his family many years before had just come to fruition.

Joseph immediately recognized his brothers, but his brothers had not recognized him. Joseph ultimately accused his brothers of being spies and sent them to jail for three days. They denied the allegations, trying to explain they were all one man's sons and there was a younger brother as well at home with their father.

On the third day Joseph said that if the brothers were telling the truth, one of them would not mind staying in jail while the others took their corn home, but then added *"... bring your youngest brother unto me; so shall your words be verified, and ye shall not die...." (Genesis 42:20)* I don't think Joseph was messing with their heads. I think in his own nonchalant way, he was just trying to find out all he could about his father Jacob and his younger brother Benjamin. I am sure that Joseph wanted to see them as well.

While the brothers discussed their situation amongst themselves and because Joseph had only spoken to them through an interpreter, they had no idea that Joseph understood every word they were saying. Reuben was reminding the others how they had treated their brother Joseph and asking how they could expect to be treated any differently. This is exactly what they had coming. As they talked of the past, Joseph *"...*

turned himself about from them, and wept; and returned to them again, and communed with them, and took from them Simeon, and bound him before their eyes." (Genesis 42:24) So with Simeon sitting in jail, the brothers left for home with corn that had cost them nothing. Unbeknownst to them, Joseph had told his servants, *"to fill their sacks with corn, and to restore every man's money into his sack, and to give them provision for the way: and thus did he unto them." (Genesis 42:25)* Now I ask you, does it sound like Joseph harbored malice or revenge in his heart for all those years? Of course not, but with our human reasoning, no one would have blamed Joseph if he had. The Bible says in *Isaiah 55:8 "For my thoughts are not your thoughts, neither are your ways my ways, saith the LORD."* Instead Joseph had compassion for his brothers.

Upon arriving home, Jacob's sons told him that the lord of the land had accused them of being spies and the only way they were going to get Simeon back was to take Benjamin to Egypt to prove they were telling the truth and truly not spies. And Jacob replied, *"...Me have ye bereaved of my children: Joseph is not, and Simeon is not, and ye will take Benjamin away: all these things are against me." (Genesis 42:36)* So Jacob made his decision: Benjamin was not going to Egypt.

"And the famine was sore in the land." (Genesis 43:1) Once again Jacob's family was in need of corn, but when Jacob told his sons he was sending them back to Egypt, Judah reminded his father, that unless Benjamin was coming with them there would be absolutely no use in going because the man had said, *"...Ye shall not see my face, except your brother be with you." (Genesis 43:5)*

The time came when Jacob told his sons, take, *"... the best fruits in the land in your vessels, and carry down the man a present, a little balm, and a little honey, spices, and myrrh, nuts, and almonds: And take double money in your hand; and the money that was brought again in the mouth of your sacks, carry it again in your hand; peradventure it was an oversight: Take also your brother, and arise, go again unto the man." (Genesis 43:11-13)*

"And when Joseph saw Benjamin with them, he said to the ruler of his house, Bring these men home, and slay, and make ready; for these men shall dine with me at noon." (Genesis 43:16)

When Joseph's brothers noticed they were being taken to the house of the second in command of all of Egypt, they began to get very nervous. I am going out on a skinny limb here and say that it was probably not common practice to be invited to the second-in-command guy's house for lunch when anyone came from the land of Canaan to buy corn.

Of course they had no idea they would be having lunch; they thought it was over the money mishap, so they started to explain, but the man at the door said, *"...Peace be to you, fear not: your God, and the God of your father, hath given you treasure in your sacks: I had your money. And he brought Simeon out unto them." (Genesis 43:23)*

When Joseph arrived home, his brothers once again bowed down before him, and they gave Joseph the gifts they had brought. Joseph not only inquired about their welfare but of their father's also. *"And they answered, Thy servant our father is in good health, he is yet alive... And he lifted up his eyes, and saw his brother Benjamin... and he sought where to weep; and he entered into his chamber, and wept there."(Genesis 43:28-30)*

When Joseph regained his composure, he returned to his brothers. Because it was an abomination to the Egyptians to eat with the Hebrew people, they ate separately; nevertheless, they still enjoyed their time together.

The next morning all eleven of Jacob's sons were on their way back home, although they had no idea that Joseph's servants had been instructed to fill each man's sack with corn and to restore each man his money. In Benjamin's case, they were to put Joseph's silver cup in the mouth of his sack.

Joseph's brothers were not very far out of the city when the steward Joseph sent overtook them and accused them of stealing. Joseph's brothers were shocked I am sure. Stealing? YIKES! And they said to the steward, *"Behold, the money, which we found in our sacks' mouths, we brought again unto thee out of the land of Canaan: how then should we steal out of thy lord's house silver or gold? With whomsoever of thy servants it be found, both let him die, and we also will be my lord's bondmen." (Genesis 44:8-9)* And the steward replied with, *"...he with whom it is found shall be my servant; and ye shall be blameless." (Genesis 44:10)*

The steward began his search, and of course, *"...the cup was found in Benjamin's sack." (Genesis 44:12)* So they turned around and returned to Joseph's house, and once again the brothers found themselves bowing down before him. Judah wanted to know if there was anything they could say or do that would clear them of the charges placed against them. Joseph said all of them were free to go, *"...but the man in whose hand the cup is found, he shall be my servant; and as for you, get you up in peace unto your father." (Genesis 44:17)* Oh boy, Judah had to have been sweating bullets by then. Go home without Benjamin, how could this be?

Judah speaking with Joseph said, *"My lord asked his servants, saying, Have ye a father, or a brother? And we said unto my lord, We have a father, an old man, and a child of his old age.... And thou saidst unto thy servants, Bring him down unto me.... And we said unto my lord, The lad cannot leave his father: for if he should leave his father, his father would die. And thou saidst unto thy servants, Except your youngest brother come down with you, ye shall see my face no more." (Genesis 44:19-23)*

Judah finally told Joseph it would cause his father's death if they came home without Benjamin and that he had told his father, *"...If I bring him not unto thee, then I shall bear the blame to my father for ever." (Genesis 44:32)* So he asked Joseph to let him stay in the place of Benjamin because they just could not stand to see the pain and sorrow it would bring to their father to lose another son.

"Then Joseph could not refrain himself before all them that stood by him; and he cried, Cause every man to go out from me. And there stood no man with him, while Joseph made himself known unto his brethren." (Genesis 45:1) Joseph cried so loud that everyone in the house could hear him. *"And Joseph said unto his brethren, Come near to me, I pray you. And they came near. And he said, I am Joseph your brother, whom ye sold into Egypt. Now therefore be not grieved, nor angry with yourselves, that ye sold me hither: for God did send me before you to preserve life."(Genesis45:4,5)*

It had been over twenty years since they had last seen Joseph. Can you imagine what a shock it was to the brothers when this apparent Egyptian man identified himself as Joseph? Yeah! Do you suppose they were thinking, *Well, the little dreamer was right; here we are bowing down to him just like he said.* The biggest shock for them must have been to see everyone but the King of Egypt bowing down to him also.

The brothers knew how heartless they had been to Joseph, yet Joseph forgave them for every lousy thing they had put him through. *"And Joseph said unto them, Fear not: for am I in the place of God? But as for you, ye thought evil against me; but God meant it unto good, to bring to pass, as it is this day, to save much people alive. Now therefore fear ye not: I will nourish you, and your little ones. And he comforted them, and spake kindly unto them." (Genesis 50:19-21)*

Joseph sent his brothers back to the land of Canaan to get their father, their families, and their cattle, and they were to return to Egypt where they would live in the land of Goshen.

When Jacob arrived in Egypt, *"Joseph made ready his chariot, and went up to meet Israel his father, to Goshen, and presented himself unto him; and he fell on his neck, and wept on his neck a good while." (Genesis 46:29)* Can you imagine what a reunion that must have been?

Because I am focusing on just one aspect of Joseph's life, may I recommend you read Genesis chapters 24 through 50 so you do not miss one a single detail of this important part of history?

Chapter 7

Forgiveness

Webster's Elementary Dictionary for Boys and Girls definition for *forgiveness* as a n.: "the act of forgiving; pardon."

Murder is committed by someone who is undoubtedly focused on satisfying himself, giving no thought to the long-term consequences that follow such a horrendous act. Murder is ruthless, destructive, and causes irreversible damage to so many, regardless of whether that murder is committed by your hands or in your heart.

"Let all bitterness, and wrath, and anger, and clamour, and evil speaking, be put away from you, with all malice: And be ye kind one to another, tenderhearted, forgiving one another, even as God for Christ's sake hath forgiven you." (Ephesians 4:31, 32) Bitterness, wrath, anger, complaining, bad mouthing and malice will cause problems in a relationship and will ultimately result in separation. If these issues are not resolved not only will these sins cause you problems they will be passed on to your children.

As a parent, I wanted to do the best I could for my children, and I believe most parents want the best for their children also. But we all make mistakes, mostly because we do not think things through before actions are put to thoughts. We just do that which seems right to us at the time, or maybe we are following the paths of our own upbringing.

I do clearly remember telling my boys that they were not born with a child-rearing manual in their hands, so mistakes would be involved. Now did I set out to destroy my children's lives? No, of course not, but I am sure they thought that was my ultimate goal. They were not free to roam the streets, nor were they allowed to say or do whatever their hearts desired.

My guys were adorable when they were little, but I did not let that deter me from making them behave themselves or holding them accountable for their actions. I was very strict with them because that is how I was raised. There was no disrespect allowed at our house. I tried to never show any type of favoritism with my children because I had witnessed the heartache and strife even just the thought of favoritism caused.

My father was born in 1925, an illegitimate child, and for the first ten years of his life was raised by his God-fearing maternal grandmother. After his grandmother's death, he lived with his mother, a step-father and half brother and sister. Of course my father felt left out and unloved compared to his siblings by the favoritism that was shown, so here is where our dysfunctional family started. My father's lack of forgiveness caused this general weakness to continue on in the lives of the next generation.

What are we teaching our children? Are we intentionally or unintentionally causing our children heartache and grief by continuing to teach them only what we learned through the heartaches of our own lives? Is it possible we are overcompensating with our children as we try to rid ourselves of our own past hurts and sorrows through guilt or confusion?

I saw myself as a strict but fair mother; I let my boys be the dictators of their own discipline. If they were well behaved, there was no need for discipline. When they were out of control or looking for new guidelines, guidance was provided and warnings were given, and if necessary discipline was enforced. If the first form of discipline did not work, a stronger discipline followed. Was I wrong or unfair? Only God knows. Was I always right? NO, perfection does not run in our family.

Forgiveness is the key that will open the door to the personal freedom you are looking for. I know forgiveness does not come easy. I have been in devastating positions a few times myself. I could see no possible way of ever forgiving the person responsible for causing my world to change forever. I agree there are some circumstances too horrible to forget, and your life may never be the same because of them; but by the grace of God, you can get through them. By that same grace, you can forgive the perpetrator. Remember you are not forgiving the sin, only the sinner. *"…My grace is sufficient for thee: for my strength is made perfect in weakness…." (2 Corinthians 12:9)* Grace is the infinite love and mercy shown to us by God upon accepting His Son Jesus Christ as your very own personal Savior, though underserved; you receive the ultimate forgiveness of all sin.

Have you accepted the Son of God as your personal Savior yet? If you have not, do you know you can accept Christ as your Savior right now, this very minute! Let me tell you how. The Bible makes it very clear. *"For God so loved the world, that he gave his only begotten Son, that whosoever believeth in him should not perish, but have everlasting life. For God sent not his Son into the world to condemn the world; but that the world through him might be saved. He that believeth on him is not condemned: but he that believeth not is condemned already, because he hath not believed in the name of the only begotten Son of God." (John 3:16-18)*

Wait, there's more: *"Jesus saith unto him, I am the way, the truth, and the life: no man cometh unto the Father, but by me." (John 14:6)*

"The Lord is…not willing that any should perish, but that all should come to repentance." (2 Peter 3:9)

"For all have sinned, and come short of the glory of God." (Romans 3:23)

"...The gift of God is eternal life through Jesus Christ our LORD." (Romans 6:23)

"For I am not ashamed of the gospel of Christ: for it is the power of God unto salvation to every one that believeth...." (Romans 1:16)

"Neither is there salvation in any other: for there is none other name under heaven given among men, whereby we must be saved." (Acts 4:12)

Now here is where you come in, *"That if thou shalt confess with thy mouth the Lord Jesus, and shalt believe in thine heart that God hath raised him from the dead, thou shalt be saved. For with the heart man believeth unto righteousness; and with the mouth confession is made unto salvation." (Romans 10:9, 10)*

Okay, now you just need to pray, confessing you are a sinner and in need of Christ as your personal Saviour. The Bible says, *"For whosoever shall call upon the name of the Lord shall be saved." (Romans 10:13)* It is very important that you notice it said, *"...shall be saved...."* It does not say "may" but *"...shall...."* The word *shall* means; "certain, without doubt, reliable and assured."

Here is the rest of the good news: you cannot lose your salvation. *"And I give unto them eternal life; and they shall never perish, neither shall any man pluck them out of my hand. My Father, which gave them me, is greater than all; and no man is able to pluck them out of my Father's hand. I and my Father are one." (John 10:28-30)*

After salvation we become a new person in Christ, *"Therefore if any man be in Christ, he is a new creature: old things are passed away; behold, all things are become new." (2 Corinthians 5:17)* You can say with confidence, *"I can do all things through Christ which strengtheneth me." (Philippians 4:13)*

I know, bad things happen to good people and good things happen to bad people, and for the life of me, I just can not wrap my simple mind around the whys. I still do not know why, but I have accepted the fact that I do not always have to have an answer to every question.

I was at a loss most of the time on how to handle the difficult situations that were constantly coming into my life, and there were plenty of them. I struggled and worried and wondered what I could do to escape the miserable life I was living, with uncertainty around every corner.

After I accepted Christ as my personal Savior and was given a brand new life, things began to change. Now it didn't happen over night because we all know old habits are hard to break; and God knows that about us, but He is very loving and patient where His children are concerned. God gives us our own free will to make our own choices; then He patiently guides us along the way.

Frustration is a feeling of disappointment and being dissatisfied because plans, hopes, or dreams have not fulfilled. Before long discouragement starts settling in, and anger is making way for bitterness, and then meanness and cruelty turn into violence. Depression and despair, despondency and gloom follow until giving up is the only thing left to do.

The Bible says, *"Train up a child in the way he should go: and when he is old, he will not depart from it." (Proverbs 22:6)* When we focus on the disappointments in life, we are training those watching to do the same. I know we do not set out each day to purposely train our children or those around us to go in the wrong direction, but actions do speak louder than words. That old saying *"Do as I say not as I do"* doesn't work any better today than it did when I was growing up. The Bible say, *"...fathers, provoke not your children to wrath: but bring them up in the nurture and admonition of the Lord." (Ephesians 6:4)*

Of course this new way of life will take faith, courage, endurance, and patience, but it will be worth it because those watching will see the changes, and will begin to change too.

Because we are all sinners, we want and need forgiveness, so it is not unreasonable that it be required of us to be forgiving of others. In *1 John 1:9* the Bible says, *"If we confess our sins, he is faithful and just to forgive us our sins, and to cleanse us from all unrighteousness." "Wherewithal shall a young man cleanse his way? by taking heed thereto according to thy word." (Psalms 119:9)*

While hanging on the Cross at Calvary, just before Jesus died for the sins of the world, He said, *"…Father, forgive them; for they know not what they do…." (Luke 23:34)*